This book belongs to

_____

_____

Welcome to my illustrated world of Fantasy Tiny Homes!

Dreaming of downsizing? Welcome to my collection of Fantasy Tiny Homes. Whimsical and wonderful, eccentric and imaginative, every illustration is a story waiting to be brought to life through color.

Inside you will find 25 original, beautifully hand-drawn illustrations to color, suitable for all skill levels. Bring your color vision to life as you explore each home and meet the quirky inhabitants.

See more at rjhampson.com

 russelljamesart

Published by Hop Skip Jump
PO Box 1324 Buderim Queensland Australia 4556

First published 2021.
Copyright © 2021 R. J. Hampson.

All Rights Reserved. Without limiting the rights under copyright reserved above, no part of this publication may be reproduced, stored in or introduced into a retrieval system, or transmitted, in any form or by any means (electronic, mechanical, photocopying, recording or otherwise), without the prior written permission of both the copyright owner and the above publisher of this book. The only exception is by a reviewer who may share short excerpts in a review.

ISBN: 978-1-922472-24-3

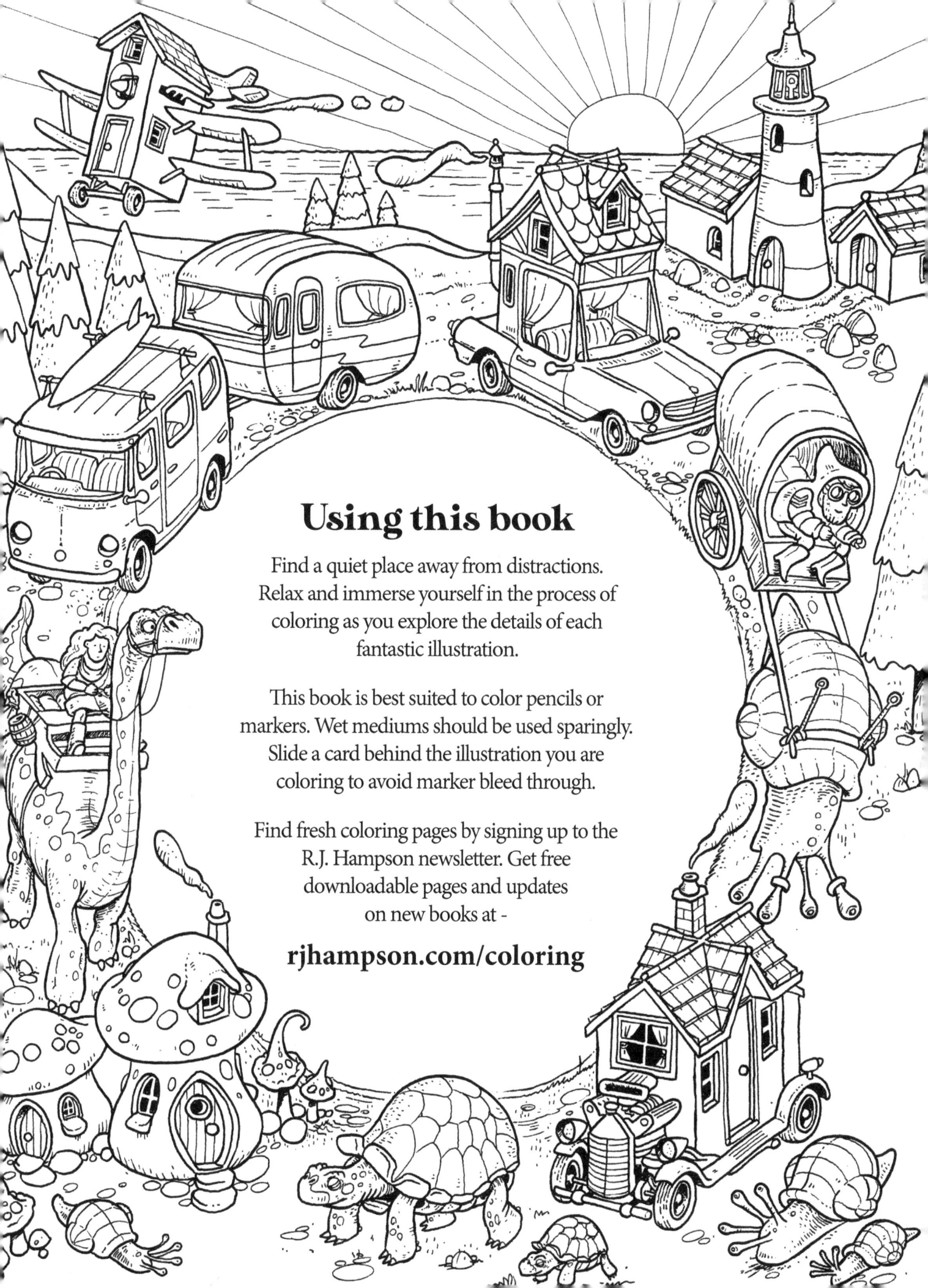

Using this book

Find a quiet place away from distractions. Relax and immerse yourself in the process of coloring as you explore the details of each fantastic illustration.

This book is best suited to color pencils or markers. Wet mediums should be used sparingly. Slide a card behind the illustration you are coloring to avoid marker bleed through.

Find fresh coloring pages by signing up to the R.J. Hampson newsletter. Get free downloadable pages and updates on new books at -

rjhampson.com/coloring

MOBILE CASTLE

SMUGGLER'S HIDEOUT

CAMPER VAN

A HOUSE IN THE WOODS

KNIGHT ERRANT

OBSERVATORY

POWERHOUSE

SMALL TUDOR BEDSIT

TORTOISE HOME

THE WAY THROUGH THE WOODS

CAT HOUSE

CAT HOUSE

GNOME HOME

FLOATING HOUSE

JUNGLE HOUSE

AIRBORNE TINY HOME

BOOT HOUSE

BOOT HOUSE

JURASSIC HOME

MOUSE HOUSE

TREE HOUSE

NAUTICAL THEMED TINY HOME

INFLATABLE TINY HOME WITH ELEPHANTS

ISLAND HOME

CANAL BOATS

CANAL BOATS

3 LITTLE HOMES

Searching for more?

Find new coloring pages by signing up to Russell's newsletter.
Get free downloadable pages and updates on new books at -
rjhampson.com/coloring

Thanks for choosing this coloring book.
If you enjoyed it, please consider leaving a review.
It will help to let more people in on the experience
plus you'd certainly make this illustrator very happy!

More books in this series

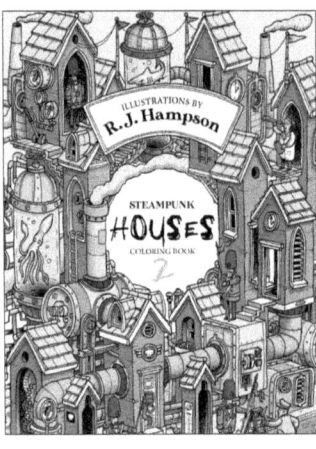

COLLECT THEM ALL!

See flip-throughs for all coloring books at **rjhampson.com**

www.ingramcontent.com/pod-product-compliance
Lightning Source LLC
Chambersburg PA
CBHW041221240426
43661CB00012B/1104